STRAIGHT FROM THE CONVENT

Borgo Press Books by CHARLES DUFRESNY

The Spirit of Contradiction & The Double Widowing: Two Plays
Straight from the Convent & The Interrupted Wedding: Two Plays (with Florent Dancourt)
The Village Coquette & The Crazy Wager: Two Plays (with Florent Dancourt)

STRAIGHT FROM THE CONVENT

& THE INTERRUPTED WEDDING: TWO PLAYS

CHARLES DUFRESNY

with Florent Dancourt;
Translated and Adapted by Frank J. Morlock

THE BORGO PRESS
MMXIII

STRAIGHT FROM THE CONVENT

Copyright © 1998, 2010, 2013 by Frank J. Morlock

FIRST EDITION

Published by Wildside Press LLC

www.wildsidebooks.com

DEDICATION

To Sandra Gulland

CONTENTS

STRAIGHT FROM THE CONVENT, with Florent Dancourt .9
CAST OF CHARACTERS. 11
THE PLAY 13
THE INTERRUPTED WEDDING 83
CAST OF CHARACTERS. 85
THE PLAY 87
ABOUT THE TRANSLATOR. 145

STRAIGHT FROM THE CONVENT
WITH FLORENT DANCOURT

CAST OF CHARACTERS

Lydia

Sybille

Letty

Noggs

Worthy

Leeson

Raddles

Fanshawe

Neville

THE PLAY

Enter Noggs coughing.

NOGGS

Hmm—hmmm—hem.

RADDLES

What an awful cold that is!

NOGGS

When this cough gets me, I have a hard time not to be carried off by it.

RADDLES

Fortunately, you're young and strong.

NOGGS

Yes, I'm young, but I've almost always got a cold. Arrh! Hem.

RADDLES

It's nothing, sir, and marriage will fix you up. Either you'll get rid of the cold, or the cold will get rid of you. There's nothing else to do. Stop in to see your betrothed while you are here; her presence alone may ease the bitterness of your cold.

NOGGS

On the contrary, c'h-hem gets worse when I'm with her. And because she's naïve, ingenuous, each time I cough, she curtsies to me as if I were sneezing, and it's useless to tell her not to—which infuriates me and makes the cough worse.

RADDLES

She's a girl who knows how to love.

NOGGS

She really has no wit, and that makes me prefer her to other women—because if I must marry hem, haar, and I feel I was born for society—

RADDLES

Right you are! At your age to live a widower!

NOGGS

My son is in the army despite me—a libertine, a wastrel who will amount to nothing, and that obliges me, in all conscience, to marry and found a family, and not let the family perish.

RADDLES

Your intentions are good, and—

NOGGS

Go say good day for me to that pretty child—

RADDLES

Come—do it yourself.

NOGGS

No—I'm going to finish coughing at my attorney's. Tell Madame Lydia I am waiting to sign the contract just as we agreed. (coughing) Go quickly! (coughing)

Hem! Haarr!

(Exit Noggs)

RADDLES

The poor old fellow with his desire to found a family!

He's clearly pressed to travel to the next world. Well—so much the worse for him. It's his business. And mine is to press my affair with Miss Letty. She's young and pretty, and marriage won't kill her—or me!

VOICE (off stage)

What a mischance!

RADDLES

I hear somebody. Let's go in and see. I'll have plenty of time to speak to Master's Lady Fair.

(Exit Raddles)

LEESON

That's very irritating.

WORTHY

Ah! How unfortunate are the children of unreasonable fathers.

LEESON

How miserable are those valets whose masters are in love.

WORTHY

What craziness of mine to be separated from London simply to go into the Army.

LEESON

What wisdom to have left the Army to return to London.

WORTHY

I am born under an unfortunate star.

LEESON

A touching affair, I admit.

WORTHY

Son of a disgustingly rich father.

LEESON

Who has reduced us by his villainy to live by our wits and on credit.

WORTHY

Oh—I skip his avarice.

LEESON

How good of you!

WORTHY

But I cannot forgive him for the despair to which he had reduced my love.

LEESON

You're right—it's unforgivable

WORTHY

In visiting a relative at the Convent, I found a young person—charming—adorable.

LEESON

You became passionately in love with her?

WORTHY

How could I help it?

LEESON

Right—how to prevent it; I would have gone mad myself.

WORTHY

I rendered her my respect.

LEESON

Nothing is more natural

WORTHY

She was aware of my tender feelings, and I got her permission to ask for her hand.

LEESON

All good so far!

WORTHY

I proposed the affair to my father.

LEESON

Here it starts to go wrong.

WORTHY

He refused to consent.

LEESON

There's malice in this, because there was no reason.

WORTHY

In despair at his refusal, I threw myself at Sybille's feet. I begged her to leave the convent and marry me secretly.

LEESON

But for the fear of her mother, it was a done deal, but mothers are troublesome creatures, rather inconvenient, especially when daughters are timid.

WORTHY

So—mad with rage and despair, I went to France to wait for the opportune moment to dispose of myself without my father's consent.

LEESON

And that moment has come. You've reached your majority—and it would be a real shame for you not to find your mistress.

WORTHY

What has become of her, my poor Leeson?

LEESON

Didn't you just say? Her mother took her out of the convent, without giving her time to even say goodbye to anybody. She's been seen in this part of town, and perhaps she lives hereabouts.

WORTHY

I will never be happy again until I've found her.

LEESON

Why not? It's nice not to have anything to reproach yourself for. Let's see. Where shall we start our search?

WORTHY

Stay here, walk around the neighborhood, and try to learn from the people around here.

LEESON

Leave it to me.

WORTHY

As for me, I will go back to the convent and get some particulars which my excitement made me forget to ask.

LEESON

Shall I wait for you here?

WORTHY

If you discover something, come quick to tell me.

(Exit Worthy)

LEESON

He's complaining and I agree. It's a sad job running after a mistress. Not the same for a woman, and, please God, that during our sojourn in France mine—who doesn't know what's become of me—has taken it in her head to quit London. I'll look for her where I won't find her. But what's this I see? I believe it's Raddles, Mr. Noggs' valet. Where did he come from, and what's he looking for in this out-of-the-way place?

(Enter Raddles)

RADDLES

Why, I believe that's Leeson.

LEESON

He's seen me. Hang on, straight face.

RADDLES

Hey, good day, Mr. Leeson, and how long have you been back? I thought you were somewhere in France.

LEESON

Peace. Pretend not to see me—I am here incognito.

RADDLES

What the devil do you mean, incognito?

LEESON

Hey, my poor boy—how wild the young are!

RADDLES

The old folks aren't far behind them.

LEESON

Well, that old boy's a strange fellow, for sure.

RADDLES

He's the most foolish fellow I have ever seen.

LEESON

Nothing's lacking—when we speak of going mad with love—for him to be the perfect model.

RADDLES

He is perfect—nothing's missing.

RADDLES

But don't let your master know anything of this.

LEESON

Fie! When did I ever tell him anything that I wasn't sure he knew anyway? Rest assured.

RADDLES

His father has taken the occasion of his absence to get married.

LEESON

Why, the old rake—to contract a clandestine marriage. And what a misfortune to the woman married to a husband of sixty-four, sickly, gouty, avaricious—and bad-tempered to boot.

RADDLES

She's a little lady who lacks the brains to realize what's happening to her, and depends on a mother who's forcing her to marry.

LEESON

Ah! Murder! And you actually permit it! You have no conscience.

RADDLES

Well, the matter's not yet settled. In the house there's a little chambermaid who doesn't like the bizarre way things are falling out, and who is taking care of the interests of the little lady despite herself.

LEESON

My word, she's a good one! She must be a maid of honor, that chambermaid. Your mistress, apparently, from the look of it—

RADDLES

Pretty question. How could it be otherwise?

LEESON

Is she much taken with your worth?

RADDLES

I'll answer you this way: the only thing holding up our marriage is the death certificate of a husband she once had. If it comes, fine—if not, we'll make do.

LEESON

That makes good sense. Is she at home?

RADDLES

Exactly. Stay here a while, then you can see our old Adonis enter.

LEESON

No—I'm afraid he might see me. And my master and I don't want him to know we are here.

RADDLES

That means there's romance in the air.

LEESON

Don't betray us.

RADDLES

I won't. Don't say anything of what I told you.

LEESON

Don't worry.

RADDLES

(aside) Let's warn the old boy his son is in London.

LEESON

Let's run to tell my master about the way his father is

carrying on.

(Exit Raddles.)

(As Leeson starts to leave, Letty enters and drags him to one side.)

LETTY

Oh, double-dog, it's you. In the end, I've caught you again after having looked so long.

LEESON

One cannot avoid one's curse. It's my wife.

LETTY

What have you done, infamous man, since you left home?

LEESON

Well, what's the matter, child, what's agitating you? If you pretend to cry, I'm leaving.

LETTY

No, traitor, you won't escape me.

LEESON

Then let's talk without getting carried away, if you don't mind.

LETTY

What a rogue—without getting carried away!

LEESON

Yes, me, I like calm talk.

LETTY

I don't know what prevents me from—

LEESON

If we don't talk quietly, the conversation will end badly, I warn you.

LETTY

To abandon your wife like this.

LEESON

Well, why complain?—you found me again.

LETTY

Leave me on the street like a beggar.

LEESON

Well—did I have any money? What do you say to that?

LETTY

To reduce me to the necessity of going into service.

LEESON

Big misfortune. Am I not in service, too? Where are you living? Look, we must come to a finish—and I'm tired of being a libertine.

LETTY

You think it's a joke, but—

LEESON

No, I'm speaking in good faith. Where do you live? Or are you homeless?

LETTY

Where do I live? I live in that house—where I endure all the trouble and shame imaginable.

LEESON

Where do you say?

LETTY

In that house.

LEESON

Wow! Oh, oh, on my word—am I lucky. And Mr. Raddles? How does he master you, I pray?

LETTY

Mr. Raddles?

LEESON

Truly, my little lady, my one and only, you are a pretty little thing.

LETTY

What are you saying?

LEESON

And the death certificate, my princess—where will you get it?

LETTY

You must be a sorcerer!

LEESON

I'm indebted to you, truly—and it was with kind intentions that you sought news of me.

LETTY

Oh, don't get carried away, I beg you. I like cool reasoning just as much as you do.

LYDIA

(off)

Letty!

LETTY

They're calling me. You're lucky I haven't got the time to have an explanation with you.

LEESON

Well, be on your way, go; we will have the time later. Suffice that I know where to find you.

(Exit Leeson.)

(Enter Lydia)

LYDIA

Who were you talking to, Letty?

LETTY

One of my cousins, madam, who came to give me news of my aunt.

LYDIA

What's my daughter doing, and why aren't you with her?

LETTY

She told me to let her alone. She's sad, and I believe to cheer her up she needs other company than mine.

LYDIA

No, everybody depresses her. It was the convent that gave her this heaviness of heart and spirit which renders her insensible to everything

LETTY

That might be, but she runs the risk of being heavy-hearted for a long time, and the husband you are giving her won't be the one to draw her away from this torpor—on my oath. A man of sixty-five years to marry a girl of sixteen. And where is the cemetery, madam?

LYDIA

He's only fifty, Letty.

LETTY

That's a trick, madam—he's shaved off more than a dozen—but even if it were true, what sense is there to give a girl like her to a man like him; what the devil are you doing to her?

LYDIA

What do you want to become of her? I love her and I don't want to thwart her—but I have no fortune to give her, and that inequality of age between Old Noggs and her will give her less pain than you might think—but she lacks the brains to recognize that.

LETTY

Yes, but, as you know, wit comes to girls—in the future she will reflect, and those tardy reflections will lead to very dangerous consequences. And who knows that she may not already have a secret inclination.

LYDIA

That cannot be. She just left the convent and knows no one at all.

LETTY

She sighs, she cries, and says not one word. Those are big signs.

LYDIA

What prevents her from telling me her thoughts?

LETTY

Young girls are not open with their mothers, madam, and the fear of appearing a little advanced for their age spoils everything.

LYDIA

My daughter is still so simple and so innocent that the word love is a name unknown to her, and she has no wit, I tell you.

LETTY

Well, it's not wit that engenders love, but love that gives birth to wit, Don't rush things. They are waiting at the attorney's—go, but don't sign anything. Let me alone with her and I will talk with her.

LYDIA

Well, try to penetrate her thoughts, and on my return give me an account.

(Exit Lydia)

(Enter Sybille)

LETTY

In what a reverie she's plunged. I expected this. She has some romance in her head.

SYBILLE

How unfortunate I am. I dare not confide my shame to anyone, and perhaps, I'll be the victim of my own timidity.

LETTY

Her mind is more occupied than mine.

SYBILLE

Oh, heaven!

LETTY

You look like you're going to cry. What makes you shake and sigh? No one knows what you want to say. Speak, we're listening.

SYBILLE

What do you want me to tell you?

LETTY

What you're thinking.

SYBILLE

I'm not thinking anything.

LETTY

Bosh! At your age there isn't a girl alive who doesn't think something.

SYBILLE

I'm not like the others.

LETTY

Listen to that, will you! But here's a strange resistance. Perhaps you think that I am indiscreet. That's what is keeping you from telling me your feelings. But I warn you that I can divine them—

SYBILLE

Then why ask me, Letty?

LETTY

To hear it from your own mouth, and to have the right to offer my humble services.

SYBILLE

And what help could you give me?

LETTY

That which you need.

SYBILLE

Still—

LETTY

Well—for example—

SYBILLE

For example, what?

LETTY

If this strange marriage your mother is determined to force on you pains you, then there are ways to be found to help you break it off.

LETTY

And what ways could you find?

LETTY

Well, for instance, if you had someone else in mind

and were to confide in me—

SYBILLE

What could you do for me?

LETTY

You want an example?

SYBILLE

Yes, yes, an example is precisely what I want.

LETTY

Don't be afraid to open your heart to me. Obviously you love someone—and is it such a shameful thing to love someone at your age? But I'd laugh at you—because you don't know what love's about.

SYBILLE

Oh, I know—don't laugh.

LETTY

Good—that pleases me. I love people who are open. Tell me everything—and hide nothing.

SYBILLE

If you want me to answer, you'll have to ask me, Letty.

LETTY

Fine. That saves modesty. First of all, I wager you love some young man.

SYBILLE

You've got it. It's Worthy.

LETTY

Worthy. Now there's a name that interests me. Does he have wit, this Worthy?

SYBILLE

I don't know enough myself to say.

LETTY

It will come, be patient.

SYBILLE

If only I had some, it would be a help, I tell you.

LETTY

You don't lack character. Let's get back to Worthy. Do

you love him a lot?

SYBILLE

Yes, I love him but I haven't heard anything from him.

LETTY

What?

SYBILLE

He's in the army—

LETTY

Well?

SYBILLE

I'm engaged to Mr. Noggs for all that—

LETTY

And?

SYBILLE

Don't ask what I am hard-pressed to tell.

LETTY

Is it that during his absence you've taken another lover?

SYBILLE

Right, again. But I'm very embarrassed, Letty.

LETTY

Well—what is it? Let's see.

SYBILLE

I've given Mr. Fanshawe a rendezvous here.

LETTY

Oh, you lucky little minx. What does Mr. Fanshawe do? After all, a lover must do something.

SYBILLE

He's a bureaucrat. But only during the day. At night he sports a sword.

LETTY

Very nice.

SYBILLE

His sister was with me in the convent, and she was the one who begged me to love him.

LETTY

It's hard to refuse a friend.

SYBILLE

If Worthy hadn't been absent, I would never have loved him.

LETTY

The absentee is always in the wrong, you are right. Now what can I do for you?

SYBILLE

And there's another problem. (hesitating) I also told Mr. Neville that he could come.

LETTY

Two of 'em! Clever work for a baby.

SYBILLE

What worries me is that I'm afraid they'll both come at the same time.

LETTY

Surely you appointed them different times?

SYBILLE

What do you want? I wasn't thinking, and fear of being Mrs. Noggs bothered me so much I didn't realize what I was doing.

LETTY

This little girl will go far!

SYBILLE

What do you say?

LETTY

Me? I was saying I will go far to help you.

SYBILLE

I'll manage if you don't abandon me.

LETTY

Abandon you? Not for my life. You worry too much.

(Enter Leeson and Worthy)

LEESON

Yes, your father's going to get married—it's no fable.

WORTHY

Let him marry a thousand times so long as I recover what I've lost.

SYBILLE

Here's someone— Let's go back in.

LETTY

Perhaps it's Neville.

SYBILLE

No, not he— What do I see?

WORTHY

Leeson, old chap, it's Sybille.

LEESON

By Jove, it is.

SYBILLE

My dear Letty, it's Worthy.

LETTY

Worthy. And what will we do with the other two?

LEESON

What's wrong: are you dumb?

WORTHY

Give me time to breathe.

LEESON

Have you lost your voice?

WORTHY

Pooh! People in love.

LETTY

You're a nice traitor and you love me to perfection.

LEESON

I loved you once, but the death certificate taught me better.

SYBILLE

Where are you coming from, Worthy? Who told you I'm to be married?

WORTHY

You're to be married, madam? Oh, just heaven! This

misadventure completes my despair.

LEESON

Wait, wait, sir—don't give way to despair. It isn't so terrible. First of all, your father is your rival.

WORTHY

My father!

LEESON

The same! Raddles told me. Raddles, by the bye, is himself going to marry my wife.

LETTY

What are you getting at?

SYBILLE

Letty is your spouse?

LEESON

Yes, ma'am; and if she can get you to become my master's wife, I'll forgive her for planning not to be mine anymore— (to Worthy) You see what I do to serve you?

WORTHY

Dear children, don't abandon us.

SYBILLE

Neville and Fanshawe are coming, Letty.

LEESON

Think how to appease me. Because, according to all the rules, I ought to be in a fury.

LETTY

Follow me inside and trust in my savoir-faire.

WORTHY

But now, what do you suggest?

SYBILLE

Do what she says, and leave me alone to manage certain things that fall to me to dispose of. (to Letty) Lock them in my room and come back to me here.

WORTHY

May I know?

LETTY

Come on, hurry—we have no time to lose.

LEESON

Contemplate how to atone for the affair of the death certificate.

LETTY

You'll be lucky if I have the patience to attend to it.

(Exit all but Sybille)

SYBILLE

(alone) Truly, having several lovers at once is embarrassing. If I'd expected Worthy to return, I wouldn't have given Neville and Fanshawe a rendezvous.

Witty girls never fall into such a trap, but it seems to me, it's a better precaution to have too many lovers than too few. Oh, well, Letty.

(Enter Letty)

LETTY

They're in your room.

SYBILLE

Did you lock them in?

LETTY

They cannot leave without me. I'd like to know—are you afraid they'll escape a second time?

SYBILLE

Fanshawe's coming, and I am happy knowing Worthy cannot listen to our conversation.

LETTY

What! You intend to keep them all?

SYBILLE

Not at all. I only thought of Fanshawe after Worthy left. Worthy has returned—and I have no more to do with Fanshawe.

LETTY

There's a kind of fidelity in this kind of inconstancy— And Neville—what will become of him?

SYBILLE

Fah. He's a child, a prodigal that I would never dream

of putting up with except for the fact I couldn't be sure of Fanshawe.

LETTY

Here's someone coming.

SYBILLE

It's Fanshawe. Let's try to get rid of him before Neville shows up.

LETTY

Hey, tell him things naturally; does a bureaucrat need much management?

SYBILLE

No, Letty. Make it bothersome. It's a sure way to finish the conversation.

LETTY

Wit isn't so lively in the country.

(Enter Fanshawe)

FANSHAWE

Now, madam, I've torn myself from the most important business, so as not to lose the favorable moment to express to you—

SYBILLE

I'm here on time as you see, but don't speak before this maid—she'll tell everything to my mother.

FANSHAWE

What constraints! Always beset by a mother, or servants

(Letty passes between them)

LETTY

Sir, if it's Madame Lydia you ask of, then it's to me you must speak. If it's Miss, then again you must speak to me.

FANSHAWE

One cannot avoid addressing you, and I am delighted to have the opportunity— (opening his purse)

LETTY

Ah! Very nice! I understand your business. There's no need to tell me what you two want, Miss. Shall I take the purse?

SYBILLE

Be careful.

FANSHAWE

What did you say?

SYBILLE

You may lose me, Fanshawe.

FANSHAWE

Be discreet, my dear child, that's all I ask.

LETTY

(to Sybille) It appears to be full.

FANSHAWE

Is it enough?

SYBILLE

This maid is not corruptible, Fanshawe.

LETTY

Heaven preserve me from being corruptible. I'd rather die. They confided you to my care, and it shall never be said that I—

FANSHAWE

Look, don't make so much noise, I beg you, and take it for love of me—

LETTY

He begs me so nicely.

SYBILLE

Are you mad?

LETTY

Fie, sir, it's not nice, nor honest for a bureaucrat to try to seduce a young woman—a soldier can get away with it, but the rest of you are supposed to be defenders of public morals, protectors of innocence. You're the first to attempt corruption. Go, I say—it's not right—and justice is injured by not making a punitive example—

FANSHAWE

Truly, this governess is rather mad—

LETTY

How mad? I am a dragon of virtue!

SYBILLE

Goodbye. I'll find a way to send you news of me.

FANSHAWE

You promise me?

SYBILLE

Enough. Goodbye, sir. Another time. And remember that Letty is incorruptible.

FANSHAWE

Rather an inconvenient virtue in a chambermaid—luckily rare.

SYBILLE

Oh, Letty, I believe Neville is here, and he and Fanshawe will meet. I'm afraid they will quarrel.

LETTY

We must put Fanshawe inside until you've given Neville his walking papers.

SYBILLE

Ha, ha! Fanshawe.

LETTY

Hey, come back. I'm not so bad as I pretend.

FANSHAWE

In fact you're very wicked.

LETTY

Not because of the money, at least.

FANSHAWE

The purse is yours.

LETTY

I won't take it. But—I'll watch it for you. Hurry inside. Go up the stairs. Things will be well. Soon you can come down.

(Exit Fanshawe)

SYBILLE

Have you lost your mind, Letty? To accept Fanshawe's purse?

LETTY

I don't know how it happened. But your Neville hasn't

come. Apparently it's fear of seeing him that made you think you saw him.

SYBILLE

No—here he is. I wasn't mistaken. It's himself.

LETTY

Uh-oh! This one doesn't look as easy to manage as the other one.

(Enter Neville)

NEVILLE

Devil take these bores. Two little dopes who lost at cards who stopped me—and why? To beg me for money that I was stupid enough to borrow from them. (to Letty) You've lost more than I did, beautiful, because they stole from you. Even though I didn't know I'd find you here, I'd destined my purse for you—

LETTY

Oh, sir—

NEVILLE

I tell you true, plague take me. Well, madam, here I am. What will become of us? I have fortune enough, I'm of distinguished nobility, and have a profession which will someday merit high employment—perhaps Prime Minister. I adore you, you love me, so let's declare ourselves. Your mother would have to be senseless not to consent to this marriage.

LETTY

He has no small opinion of himself.

SYBILLE

Letty, my mother is soon going to return. Make sure she doesn't surprise us.

LETTY

My word, Miss, I can say nothing. The surest way would be to separate you, and to take a long absence—so you could meet at leisure.

SYBILLE

She's right. You were very late coming. I fear my mother will find us together.

NEVILLE

Oh, pooh! Mothers of today are nothing much to be frightened of.

LETTY

Oh, there are mothers and there are mothers, sir, and the mere sight of a man's hat or a blushing face would be enough for this one to justify the most terrible actions against her daughter.

NEVILLE

Poor woman. Is she so unworldly? To judge people by their clothes. The most modest are not the least dangerous. But let's speak frankly—because I'm a philosopher. This mother that is feared so much: you shouldn't fear her without reason. Tell me—do I have a rival who can use her maternal power to force you to marry him? Don't hesitate to tell me; he won't be murdered, I promise you. I am prudent and I don't like trouble. His ears will suffice me.

LETTY

Nothing more true, and you judge rightly; after an assurance of this sort, no mystification is involved.

SYBILLE

Oh, Letty, there are dangerous people in the world.

LETTY

Only experience teaches who they are.

NEVILLE

You hesitate to answer me, and you consult. The wind is unfavorable to me. But I have a mere bagatelle to offer. I'm devilishly in love with you. And without a doubt, I'm not the only one. In a moment of anger against a more fortunate suitor, you said to yourself: let Neville come. The anger is over, you are furious to have agreed to my coming. I understand quite perfectly. But—I'll find out who he is and he'll answer to me for all this—on my honor!

LETTY

Here's Mr. Noggs.

SYBILLE

Ah, heaven.

NEVILLE

What—what is it? What's wrong with you.

(Enter Noggs and Raddles)

NOGGS

A young man with Sybille.

RADDLES

Don't cough, you'll irritate them.

SYBILLE

My dear Letty—

NEVILLE

My anger moves you—that's something. Goodbye, madam, I abandon you to your thoughts. I carry a sword—and sometimes a pistol. Let heaven fall on me if this comedian doesn't perish by my hand!

(He exits with a threatening gesture.)

RADDLES

Rest easy. He wasn't saying sweet nothings to her.

LETTY

He heard the end of the conversation.

SYBILLE

Luckily. Oh, sir, you here? If you had come but a few minutes earlier you would have had a real fright.

NOGGS

What happened to you? Speak!

SYBILLE

Give me time to compose myself—

NOGGS

Well? What is this adventure, Letty?

LETTY

What is it? Ask her, ask herself. She can explain it to you better than I can.

NOGGS

Well?

SYBILLE

I just saved the life of a young man that they planned to kill before my very eyes.

NOGGS

How the devil?

LETTY

What led him to us?

SYBILLE

Luckily, I had time to save him in my house.

NOGGS

You've done well.

LETTY

(aside) The cunning little minx!

SYBILLE

Without my help he was a dead man— No question!

LETTY

It was impossible for him to escape.

SYBILLE

Heaven brought you here to finish what we have begun.

NOGGS

How's that?

SYBILLE

Sir, if you will, it's necessary for you to escort this poor fellow, and not leave him until you've found a safe place for him.

NOGGS

A safe place?

SYBILLE

Yes, sir, I entreat you.

LETTY

(aside) Trickery is natural to her.

NOGGS

A safe place! But, if he's in your home, let him stay there—why expose him?

SYBILLE

What, sir, let him stay here! Heavens! A man hidden in my house without the knowledge of my mother! No, sir, I beg you most urgently—so she doesn't learn of this.

NOGGS

Poor child! Her simplicity charms me.

LETTY

Her scruples over these matters surpass the imagination.

NOGGS

Go, go, pretty one, nothing wrong in it, and I will explain to your mother the innocence of your action.

SYBILLE

Eh, if you love me, don't refuse what I ask. I have a thousand reasons to wish it.

LETTY

Come, sir, a little complaisance. Young people are embarrassed over the most innocent things. I will go bring him out.

NOGGS

Come on, then—I'll wait here.

RADDLES

You will make us furiously protect him.

LETTY

Shut up or watch your eyes!

RADDLES

I am a good prince. And what about the death certificate?

LETTY

It's here. But be wise.

(Exit Letty)

SYBILLE

You seem to be dreaming—what's the matter?

NOGGS

Me! Nothing's wrong. But I think you just set me a useless task, and one not suitable to my age. Me, serve as an escort to a young man?

RADDLES

It would be more natural if he served you—but at the same time— The first time someone tried to kill you—

NOGGS

Raddles.

RADDLES

Sir?

NOGGS

Don't leave me, at least.

RADDLES

I won't. I will escort the escort.

(Enter Letty and Fanshawe)

LETTY

Don't forget that in making your escape that she saved your life, and that you are with her uncle, who doesn't listen to reason on the subject of his niece.

FANSHAWE

But when can I hope?

LETTY

Let me manage it.

FANSHAWE

(to Sybille) Madam, I don't know how to repay this important service.

LETTY

Again? No ceremony. Lead them off, Mr. Raddles. They can compliment each other on the way.

RADDLES

She's right. While there's something to be done, do it. Get ready. Let the gentleman go first, you follow him, and I will be the rear guard.

FANSHAWE

Goodbye, Madam.

NOGGS

Don't stay too far apart.

RADDLES

Don't worry. Here's an order of battle.

(All exit but Letty and Sybille)

LETTY

Now we are free of those bores, but your mother won't be long coming back. What are we to do with our prisoners? We must decide something.

SYBILLE

That's why I need your advice, my dear Letty. You know—

LETTY

Yes, I know the advice you need. Your mother is a good person, tell her the tenderness you have for Worthy, cry, beg, fall at her knees. She won't be strong enough to resist your tears.

SYBILLE

And I am not strong enough to do such a thing.

LETTY

Oh, well—I will speak for you. She's coming; here's the key to your room. Go meet with your lover and leave it to me to take care of your business.

(Exit Sybille)

LETTY

(to Lydia who enters) Long life, madam. I have penetrated the secrets of your daughter. I know the cause of her shame, and if you are still in the mood not to contradict her, you will be the happiest mother in the world.

LYDIA

Meaning, Letty?

LETTY

That she hates Mr. Noggs to a wonder, and that if ever she becomes his wife, she will know how to punish him for having married her—Lord have mercy.

LYDIA

You are telling me things about my daughter.

LETTY

Oh, madam, if she's given a husband she loves, I am confident of her virtue, but with Old Noggs, I couldn't answer for hers or mine.

LYDIA

Bring her down, Letty. I want to hear this from her own mouth.

LETTY

But, madam, with all her wit she will hardly be able to explain unless you urge her on a little.

LYDIA

Let her come. I will do what is necessary.

LETTY

Things are going well.

(Exit Letty)

LYDIA

My decision is taken. I will not authorize anything my daughter does not want, and if someday she is not content, at least she won't be able to accuse me of having sacrificed her happiness to my headstrong will or to avarice.

(Enter Noggs and Raddles)

RADDLES

Well, sir, here we are back again, and we did a good deed—as you see.

NOGGS

Quiet. Here's Mrs. Lydia—I waited for you a long time at my attorney's, madam, but impatience—

LYDIA

You left just before I arrived. But I've just found reason to console myself for not having found you.

NOGGS

What reason, madam?

LYDIA

You are going to know all. You're a gallant man and will take things properly.

RADDLES

Here's a speech that says something and nothing good.

(Enter Sybille and Letty)

LETTY

You have only to speak, I tell you.

SYBILLE

But, Letty.

LYDIA

Come here, Sybille, and don't hide anything. You have no reason to complain of my manners, and you don't need to fear violence because I don't believe in it.

SYBILLE

Before I reply, permit me—

NOGGS

What is all this ceremony, madam—I watch, I hear, but I don't understand.

SYBILLE

Sir—it's that I don't love you, and mother has the goodness to want me to tell you so.

NOGGS

What, madam—you authorize a speech of this sort on the terms on which we now stand?

LYDIA

What do you want, sir? I thought my daughter's feelings agreed with mine, and I was deceived. Would you make her unhappy by forcing her inclination?

NOGGS

Would she be unhappy in marrying me?

SYBILLE

Oh, as to that, yes, sir. I swear to you we'd never be happy with each other.

LETTY

This little girl has some wit, and if you marry her, I guarantee that you will see it a hundred times more—to its advantage.

NOGGS

Well, better now than later. Still, she's under obligations to me.

LETTY

Yes, but beware the repayment. London girls push things a little far sometimes.

LYDIA

You see, sir, that my daughter—

SYBILLE

Mother, I will do what you command me, but I don't consent to the gentleman's wish that you command me to be his wife.

NOGGS

Raddles?

RADDLES

My word, sir, if I were in your place I wouldn't get on my high horse.

SYBILLE

I will satisfy my duty as a daughter in obeying you, and I will fulfill my duty as a wife by heaping all imaginable shame on my husband.

RADDLES

Sir, no use coughing, she won't curtsy to you.

LETTY

You need a woman without any pride—this one's not for you.

SYBILLE

Why, Letty? It's not pride but the natural antipathy and repugnance I have for the gentleman.

RADDLES

Of all her good qualities, remaining an ingénue isn't one of them.

NOGGS

But, madam—

LYDIA

After this, sir, you can see that it doesn't seem right to—

NOGGS

But, madam—

LETTY

Trust me, sir, don't put us to the necessity of deceiving you. You would believe yourself Milady's husband, whereas in fact, you would really be her Master of Ceremonies. For example, the young man you just escorted so handily—

NOGGS

Well—this young man I just escorted?

LETTY

He's one of your rivals. Would you have believed it?

LYDIA

What's this?

LETTY

(to Lydia) Don't get upset. It's nothing.

NOGGS

What! This young man was in love with you?

SYBILLE

Yes, sir, and I am very obliged to you for the care you took of him.

NOGGS

Oh, I am furious. What effrontery!

LETTY

Oh, don't get angry, sir. You don't know the half of it. That red-faced bully who appeared so brutal to you—!

NOGGS

Well?

LETTY

Another one.

SYBILLE

Wouldn't you have escorted him home, too, sir, if I had

asked you?

LETTY

Nice question. He's the nicest man in the world, is Mr. Noggs.

NOGGS

Oh—I think you'll soon see otherwise in what follows.

LETTY

And we still have in Miss's room a young man and his valet.

LYDIA

What! My daughter with a man in her room!

SYBILLE

She doesn't know what she's saying, Mother.

NOGGS

It will be necessary to explore this affair further, madam—to get a little light.

LETTY

You will see a young man, I tell you, newly arrived

from the army who had no room ready. You will have the goodness to fix up a room for him in your home.

NOGGS

What do you mean: in my home?

LETTY

Yes, sir, if you can escort the others, you can at least do that for this one. It's true, at least: I'm going to make you do it.

RADDLES

This will be a curious thing to see.

(Exit Letty)

LYDIA

Is it possible, daughter, that you have so far forgotten yourself —?

SYBILLE

Don't condemn me unheard, mother; two words will suffice to excuse me,

NOGGS

Plague. Such innocence! From what devil have I been

delivered?

(Enter Worthy and Leeson)

WORTHY

Father, I appear before you humbly.

LYDIA

His father!

NOGGS

Indeed, yes, madam, it's my son.

RADDLES

I told you he had come back.

LYDIA

What's he doing here, sir?

NOGGS

What's it all mean?

RADDLES

Sir, you wish to remarry to found a family—your son will do a better job of it.

LYDIA

What's your decision, sir?

NOGGS

My decision, madam, is that they marry quickly—they'll go well together, at least it will be a splendid household.

WORTHY

Oh, father, how much I owe you.

NOGGS

Don't bother to thank me.

LETTY

Oh! He doesn't know how to live the way you do, and doesn't escort people.

NOGGS

Shut up, impudence. You'll be thrown out, and I wish that was article one of the contract.

WORTHY

May I flatter myself, madam?

LYDIA

My daughter loves you and that satisfies me. May you be happy for a long time.

RADDLES

And now, Letty, as for our marriage.

LETTY

Here's the certificate that's come. There's nothing to be done.

RADDLES

What?

LEESON

Yes, my dear Raddles. I certify to you, by the grace of God, I'm fine, and that for my sins, this is my wife.

RADDLES

What! She's your wife!

LEESON

Yes, my boy. I wish it was lawful for me to defer in your favor. I would willingly pay the expense of the marriage. My word, I believe I'd be better off for it.

CURTAIN

THE INTERRUPTED WEDDING

CAST OF CHARACTERS

The COUNT

The COUNTESS

ADRIEN, Count's servant

NANETTE

DORANTE, lover of NANETTE

LUCAS, fiancé of NANETTE

Lucas' MOTHER

The SOLDIER, Lucas' Uncle

A SCRIVENER

A MUSICIAN

Violin Players

THE PLAY

SCRIVENER

Damnation, are the Count and Countess playing games—making a man like me wait so long!

LUCAS

Ah, respect, respect, Mr. Scrivener.

SCRIVENER

Damn—if the Count is the Lord of this village, I am the Royal Notary.

LUCAS

But, Mr. Scrivener, since my mother put her name there, I will do the marrying—what's the hangup?

MOTHER

Be quiet, simpleton. What's the hangup? What's the hangup!

SCRIVENER

All that remains is for this woman to subscribe now—why are we making difficulties over trifles?

MOTHER

What do you mean over trifles?

SCRIVENER

Yes, surely over trifles—over mere nothings.

MOTHER

Is a daughter's dowry nothing? The goddaughter of the Countess has only the eight hundred francs that the Count promised her. The money hasn't come and you call that a trifle?

SCRIVENER

What's it matter? Sign anyway.

MOTHER

Sign anyway—sign anyway. What do you say to that, my brother the corporal—sign anyway?

SOLDIER (nearly drunk)

Oh, hush—peace. Let me hear myself think. Sign

anyway—no money. That's as if one were to say—drink anyway. Come on, pal, drink anyway. But, there is no wine. That doesn't matter—drink anyway. So, you have to see the wine first—and then drink.

MOTHER

That's a beautiful thought. We must see the money first and then sign.

SOLDIER (pouring some wine in his glass and drinking)

You must see the wine and then drink. (pouring again and drinking) You must see the wine and then drink—beautiful thought!

SCRIVENER (also having some wine)

I, too, prefer beautiful thoughts, and especially for the completion of business. I issue a summons.

SOLDIER

And sin, repent, and relapse.

SCRIVENER

Is that a beautiful thought again?

SOLDIER

Yes—it's that you're an idiot to speak of business while I'm drinking. So, as for me, I want to drink with music. Musician, play us an air—something brisk.

MUSICIAN

Grave or gay? Quick or slow? What measure would you like?

SOLDIER

What measure would I like? I want the measure of St. Denis. That's the best.

MUSICIAN

I know an old song that suits a wedding. It talks of love, of wine and money.

MOTHER

Of money—that's good.

LUCAS

Ah, of love.

SOLDIER

The wine will be for me.

MUSICIAN (singing)

Money, love and wine

Swore a triple alliance.

They lend each other a hand.

Love is thirsty

And holy wine

Gives love strength

And confidence.

MOTHER

God be thanked. Here comes the money.

(Enter Adrien.)

MOTHER

Greetings to the Count's manager. He is going to reckon with us, reach an agreement, and deliver us.

ADRIEN (in an old livery cloak)

Didn't the Count promise you eight hundred pounds?

MOTHER

Eight hundred pounds, yes.

ADRIEN

Eight hundred pounds—good.

SCRIVENER

Is that currency?

ADRIEN

It's good, I tell you. The Count has left the disposition to me. But, our finances are short. The sale of his fruits has not taken place. There's no funds in our coffers. There are only apples.

MOTHER

I really suspected that the money wasn't coming.

ADRIEN

I give you a choice. Take the apples or the Count's word. We have no other funds.

MOTHER (grabbing the wine bottles)

There are no funds. I'm taking back my wine.

A RELATIVE (taking the pate)

No funds?

ANOTHER RELATIVE (taking the tablecloth)

No funds.

SCRIVENER (taking his books)

No funds.

MUSICIAN (putting away his music and instruments)

No funds? No music.

MOTHER

Come, Corporal, that's enough to drink. There are no funds, there will be no wedding.

SOLDIER

No wedding—by damn! I'm going to sleep on an empty stomach. Grab the bottles! Look here, Mr. Man of Affairs, bring the fiancée here. I order you to perform the wedding—or I'll bury somebody.

MOTHER

No, Brother. Do you want your nephew to marry a girl without money?

SOLDIER

I don't care about money. It's enough he's my nephew—and I will make him my heir.

MOTHER

Your heir! You don't have anything.

SOLDIER

Right. And I owe something, but my valor and my fame are nothing to anyone. Go, Lucas, you will have my soldier's commission. I will give you the survivor's benefit.

(Adrien wants to lead off Nanette, but the Soldier makes her return.)

SOLDIER

Come, give each other the marriage kiss.

MOTHER

But, Brother, be reasonable, modesty.

SOLDIER

Modesty—that's right. Give him nothing but your hand to kiss. There's nothing for modesty to fear in that.

MOTHER

But, Brother—

SOLDIER

Kiss her hand or I'll kill you.

LUCAS

Get this nonsense out of his head or he'll kill me.

SOLDIER

Oh, they're going to marry. There will be a wedding. Hurray! While we're waiting, let's go drink.

MOTHER

Come away, come away.

(The Mother leads off Lucas, and all the rest follow except Nanette, who remains with Adrien.)

ADRIEN

Goodbye, wedding, your servant— Well, Miss Fiancée, will you be mute for a long while more? The wedding behind you, the breakoff doesn't make you more gay? What's the matter with you then?

NANETTE (sighing)

Ahh.

ADRIEN

Sighing! As little as I press you, you are going to confess everything to me—for you are the exact age to be in love, and you are too young to know how to hide your love. You are blushing!

NANETTE

Ah, my poor Adrien, how a girl suffers when she dares not speak. I've been dying of desire since yesterday. I am choking with it.

ADRIEN

Why don't you ease this oppression by talking?

NANETTE

Now that the marriage is broken off I will tell the rest. But, to whom can I confide, having neither mother nor father? The Countess no longer loves me because her husband likes me too well. I hate him too much to ask his advice—and there's no girl in this here village who's cunning enough to be my confidante.

ADRIEN

Sorry my name's not Lisette or Maggie, but since the Countess has no chambermaid other than myself—I am entitled to the confidence of her goddaughter. Speak.

NANETTE

I am going to tell you my story. The other day as I was walking by myself in the little woods, I noticed a man on our wall. He fell into the alley. At first I was afraid. But no sooner had I looked at him, I confess to you, I was no longer in fear of him. Still, I reflected, I, wise girl, ought to flee. I wanted to run.

ADRIEN

And your legs failed you?

NANETTE

Perhaps so, indeed—but what stopped me was that he called to me in a languishing voice: "Ah, charming person, take pity on me. I am wounded." Indeed, I thought he had done it deliberately, but I didn't leave without having compassion. He uttered a heavy sigh. His head fell on the grass as if he were dead.

ADRIEN

And, what did the defunct say to you?

NANETTE

I was going to question him on the subject of his death, but he fled into the depths of the forest—and because the Count was coming down another path, I fled too—and because the Count is so desirous of being alone with me, I always am afraid he might find me.

ADRIEN

And, as you fled, weren't you hiding by the side of the dead man?

NANETTE

Assuredly not. I haven't seen him since. But he writes me such tender letters with all his might that I've been patient enough to reread five or six times.

ADRIEN

Here's a girl who loves to read.

NANETTE

I read his letters with pleasure—but still, to write tenderly, to die, to scale a wall—is not really enough to make an honest man. What do you make of it?

ADRIEN

Before saying anything about it, I want to tell you about

an adventure I had. Yesterday evening, as I returned to the Château, I noticed a man in the woods running after me, all out of breath. Unable to speak, he gesticulated, and in gesticulating, he put several gold crowns in my hand. Ah, sir, I said to him—if your voice is as eloquent as your gesture, you will persuade me of whatever you like. Indeed, he persuaded me that he loves you and concluded that he would ask you of the Count and Countess. Easy, I said to him. They are a couple of ferocious beasts, incapable of listening to reason. They call each other honey—sweetie—and they are two pit bulls who show their teeth twenty times a day. All their conversations begin with caresses and end in fisticuffs. I told him enough to hang our master, and I didn't tell him a quarter of the truth. As to the rest, I found out about this nice young man—his name is Dorante. He is rich, very witty, generous, polite—he is. But the Count and Countess are coming. Go wait for me down there. I will finish the portrait of Dorante for you.

(Exit Nanette.)

ADRIEN

Now, how am I going to explain to this brute that the match is broken off? He's going to blame me because they won't take his word as cash.

COUNT (to Countess as they enter)

Yes, surely. Nanette's wedding leads me to the idea of ours. How long has it been, my heart? It's been thirty-five years we've been making each other happy.

COUNTESS

If I were to consult my conjugal affection, it's only a day since I possessed you.

COUNT

In the happiness of a perfect union, the length of years is imperceptible.

COUNTESS

I observe it in your extreme politeness.

COUNT

Your complacency is extraordinary. Ah, I'm looking for you, Adrien.

ADRIEN

Here I am, sir.

COUNT

Go quick and saddle my mare. I'll go hunt up some

game for the wedding.

COUNTESS

I'm the one who needs you, Adrien. Come dress me for the wedding.

COUNT (sweetly)

But, my amiable Countess, you had a serving woman who was yours alone. She left you. Adrien belongs to me alone.

COUNTESS

Don't I have to dress up, my dear Count?

COUNT

Doesn't my horse have to be saddled?

COUNTESS

Speak to me, Adrien. I left on my dresser the curling iron for my hair. What did you do with it?

ADRIEN (pulling the iron from his pocket)

Here it is. I took it to have it soldered by our marshal.

COUNT

Oh, when the marshal has shod my horse, he will work for you. Don't bother him anymore, Madame, you always prevent service from being done.

COUNTESS

He ought to be serving me.

COUNT

After me, my love.

COUNTESS

He will do my hair—or I'll give him twenty slaps.

COUNT

He will obey me, my heart, or I'll break his arms.

ADRIEN

Ah, sir, consider that I am your only servant. I cannot, at the same time, be in the room and the stable, in the kitchen and the office, in Madame's bed and with the horse. I cannot serve three masters at once. But, happily, I shall get out of the affair today by obeying neither of you.

COUNTESS

What's it mean?

COUNT

What is it?

ADRIEN

I'll explain. You don't need to ride the horse. Madame doesn't need to dress up—for the wedding won't take place.

COUNT

The wedding won't take place! Didn't I invite the Notary and all Lucas' relatives?

ADRIEN

Yes, sir. The contract was prepared, the relatives in agreement. The violins tuned up, too. The table set, the wine poured. They only were waiting for your eight hundred francs. I offered them your word and on your word—they all disappeared.

COUNTESS

What then, knave? They didn't—?

ADRIEN

It's not my fault. They didn't want it.

COUNT

They didn't want to rely on my word, Mr. Rogue?

ADRIEN

As for me, I'm not them.

COUNT

Isn't my word good, dog face?

ADRIEN

It's not me, I tell you. You know very well I rely on your word. And you've never paid me my wages except verbally.

COUNTESS

These relatives are, indeed, insolent not to trust the word of their Lord, of their master who can ruin them with his power.

COUNT

It's because this fool didn't speak as he should. Ah, I see Lucas. I am sure that with a single word I'll make him consent to the marriage.

COUNTESS

Let's go speak to him.

(The Count and Countess go out.)

ADRIEN (alone)

All is lost. They are going to force Lucas to renew the wedding. Can't I find some expedient way to break it? Wait! The Countess is jealous of Nanette. Let's try to ignite that jealousy again, so that—

COUNTESS (returning)

I've come back, Adrien. I've come back to speak to you while my spouse is shut up with Lucas.

ADRIEN

I have, also, something to tell you that it is not good for the Count to hear. You know, Madame, that I always take your side against him in the little domestic squabbles which mix from time to time with your caresses.

COUNTESS

I get you. You want to speak of Nanette. It's about her, too, that I've come to consult you—and I absolutely intend to put that little creature a long way off. Not that

I suspect the fidelity of the Count. He's very passionately in love with me.

ADRIEN

Your presence inspires him with so much love that he will never caress Nanette in front of you. But, as soon as your back is turned, he forgets your charms.

COUNTESS

It's too much to say he forgets—rather, he has too much good taste.

ADRIEN

Agreed. To prefer youth to true beauty—to complete beauty—but he's found you beautiful for a long while, and only that Nanette is pretty.

COUNTESS

Whatever may be the case, it is good to foresee things so as to fear them less—and this marriage will ease my mind, for Lucas will take Nanette a long way off.

ADRIEN

The Count made you believe that so as not to alarm you. But I am warning you that the day after the wedding he will make Lucas his farmer and Nanette his concierge.

COUNTESS

Nanette his concierge! The traitor! The perjurer! The rogue—he must have lost his mind; it's I who must dispose of Nanette. Her father left her to me when he died. She's my goddaughter. Am I not right, my poor Adrien, am I not right?

ADRIEN

The issue is not about being right. Right is often on the side of the weakest—and it's as if it were wrong—but Madame, allow me to see if I cannot adroitly discourage Lucas from marrying Nanette. If Lucas has the courage to refuse her—you back Lucas and I will back you.

COUNTESS

No treating with a traitor! Not when I see plainly that a matchless spouse wants to have it both ways. I cannot contain myself. I am going to openly oppose this marriage and put my goddaughter in a convent.

(Exit the Countess.)

ADRIEN (alone)

Nanette in a convent! That would be a nuisance. For no Nanette for Dorante, no fortune for me—but, let's begin by breaking off this marriage. Let's go consult with Dorante.

(Enter Dorante.)

ADRIEN

Yes. Are you appearing here? You are chancing being seen. Why don't you wait for me at the rendezvous?

DORANTE

Impatience overcame me. But no one can surprise us. I've locked the doors. Tell me, Adrien, has the lovable Nanette understood my letters? Have you spoken to her of my passion? Does she listen to you, does she respond, can I hope?

ADRIEN

She understood your letters. I've spoken. She listened to me, and yet I see no great hope for you.

DORANTE

No great hope! She's insensible to my love?

ADRIEN

That's not the problem. I suppose, just to make matters brief—that she's as crazy as you—but things are not far advanced. I've already told of the Count's love, or rather, his lust for Nanette and the jealousy of the Countess, for either the wife will shut her in a convent for her own purposes, or the husband will marry for his—to a fool.

DORANTE

The Count, you say, wants to see Nanette married?

ADRIEN

To a peasant.

DORANTE

Very nice.

ADRIEN

To a fool.

DORANTE

So much the better.

ADRIEN

So much the worse, really.

DORANTE

Is this all I have to fear?

ADRIEN

Isn't it enough?

DORANTE

I only feared the indifference of Nanette. If she loves me, my happiness is assured.

ADRIEN

I don't understand you.

DORANTE

Yes, Adrien, according to the plan I've formed, the jealousy of the Countess and the evil intentions of the Count will serve to make my plans succeed. I claim that the Count will beg me to marry Nanette and the Countess will be ravished.

ADRIEN

I see there lots of impossibilities without finding a way to make a married couple who've been contradicting each other for forty years want the same thing.

DORANTE

I am going to explain my plan to you. I know that, first of all, that I have the talent to be a fine actor, and here is the role I will play.

ADRIEN

They're opening that door. Go out the other way and

go wait for me in the woods.

(Exit Dorante by one door. Enter the Count by another, followed by Lucas.)

COUNT

Adrien, do you know how my wife has been able to guess my plans?

ADRIEN

She must have read in your eyes that you wanted to make Nanette concierge and that—

COUNT (gesturing that Lucas is there)

Hush.

ADRIEN

I was wrong. I didn't see the future.

COUNT (to Lucas)

If I wanted to establish Nanette, it's because her late father served me so well.

ADRIEN (making a sign to Lucas)

You love the father, you provide for the daughter. It's natural.

COUNT

Whatever the case may be, I laugh at my wife's anger, and from this morning I am concluding the business. Adrien, get the Notary to return and all the guests for the wedding. Prepare, also, for the feast. In the villages, one can eat only what one has—my huntsman has only killed some hares today. Put two or three in the soup. Marinate them, fricassee them, in short, disguise them cleverly. Compose a diversified meal—a perfect supper.

ADRIEN

I will put your hares in four different entrees. I will even make stews for the fruit.

(Exit Adrien.)

COUNT

Don't doubt, Lucas, despite my wife. I will make you my farmer. It's enough that you and I are in agreement.

LUCAS

Yes, but the thing is, I am not in agreement.

COUNT (in a tone of authority)

Excuse me, Mr. Lucas?

LUCAS

I know your will is always in agreement with whatever you want, but as for myself, I said that to take a woman with nothing—and a farm that's worth nothing—that's too much to take in one day.

COUNT

With regard to my farm, I give you my word. That suffices.

LUCAS

That suffices! That suffices—because I don't deign to contradict you. All my wealth is in your domain. You can ruin me, but when one takes a farm, it's not to ruin oneself.

COUNT

Nor is it to strike it rich. Still, I will augment your share with strong seignoral rights, quit rents, rents and reversions—some fowl that are due me from the vassals—you'll only give me some fat capons.

LUCAS

I will give you fat capons for skinny fowl.

COUNT

You will have the added right of fishing in my lake for frogs and you will furnish me some fish.

LUCAS

Fish for frogs! I thank you for all that, and for putting in the proposed lease all the ceremonies you could think of to put to profit all the good holidays in the Almanac—for the wine of St. Martin, three hogsheads of cider—six pounds of oats for your Twelfth Night calves—two pigs for the Countess' needles, and all because you think I am anxious. But I prefer to lose it all and my love in the bargain than to sign my ruin.

COUNT

There, there, take it easy. Since you are so grasping, so hard, we'll sweeten things up a bit. Don't worry about a thing. Only think of Nanette. She's a treasure. Go to her quickly and give her your word again. I am going to conquer my wife.

(Exit Count.)

LUCAS (alone)

He's a tyrant, is this Count. He's a tyrant like Nanette who tyrannizes over my mind and, perhaps, even worse is coming—for Adrien was trying to tell me something. I've got to have a chat with him.

(Enter Adrien.)

ADRIEN

Well, pal Lucas, is your marriage settled?

LUCAS

Oh, so, so.

ADRIEN

Meaning he's going to make you marry the farm whether you like it or not, and that you'll take Nanette on lease, for the Count retains the property to himself.

LUCAS

Nothing to gain on this farm. There's nothing to lose on Nanette, is there?

ADRIEN

So, you're going to end up marrying?

LUCAS

I'm afraid the Count has started it. Quite frankly, I am really annoyed to be in love. My mother always said I would never be anything but a fool.

ADRIEN

That's what I was telling you as well.

LUCAS

Huh?

ADRIEN

No joking there—for in the end, Nanette is wise—but the Count is a bit licentious.

LUCAS

In good conscience, Mr. Adrien, Nanette hasn't given herself up to the lust of the Count, has she? For I've noticed he's in such a hurry to marry her—such a hurry.

ADRIEN

He's calculated that he must date your marriage from today. A few days sooner or later sometimes decides the reputation of a newly married woman. The world is punctilious on the date of the marriage.

LUCAS

I understand that date—

ADRIEN

It's not as I told you that Nanette is not very wise. But the Count is a careful calculator. Don't rush to any conclusion.

LUCAS

Damn. I would be of a mind to wait eight or nine months to see. But still, I have such an eye to her beauty that I don't want to wait.

ADRIEN (noticing Nanette)

I see her coming. Flee, weak Lucas, flee.

LUCAS

I'm trying to, but love takes death in its teeth. Zounds, love lied about it. I am running away. You tell the Count I want some time to think about it.

(Exit Lucas. Enter Nanette.)

NANETTE

I am in despair, my poor Adrien. The Count insists that I marry Lucas. The Countess wants to place me in a convent—and, as for me, I want something entirely different.

ADRIEN

Dorante and I have just decided that you ought to marry. The Count wants you to marry a peasant and we consent to it.

NANETTE

What do you mean?

ADRIEN

I proposed to him the other day a farmer from amongst my relatives. He's just arrived. He is jocular, young, well-built.

NANETTE

What balderdash are you telling me?

ADRIEN

I am sure he won't displease you.

NANETTE

Are you speaking seriously?

ADRIEN

Very seriously.

NANETTE

Don't you know that I would die rather than belong to anyone other than Dorante?

ADRIEN

Come, come. See my peasant.

NANETTE

I don't want to see him.

(Enter Dorante, disguised.)

ADRIEN

He's coming now.

NANETTE

Leave me alone.

ADRIEN

Look at him carefully.

NANETTE

Ah, it's Dorante.

DORANTE

Yes, charming Nanette, it's he who adores you.

ADRIEN

You know why he's disguised, but repeat what you just told me: that you would die rather than belong to anyone but Dorante.

DORANTE (transported, kissing her hand)

You said that?

NANETTE

I didn't say a thing.

ADRIEN

You didn't say anything either when he kissed your hand.

NANETTE (pulling away her hand)

You are wrong, sir, to take my hand without asking me. Do you love me enough so I can forgive you? You don't say a word. Are you afraid of lying?

ADRIEN

Silent love is love that lies least.

DORANTE

I have too much pleasure to be able to speak. You want to belong to me? Oh, repeat that, I beg you. Speak.

NANETTE

Alas, I am almost as mute as you.

ADRIEN

I foresee you will often have silent conversations. Think about it, but hurry up. Think of the role you must play with the Count. I am going to inform the Countess of our plan.

NANETTE

Ah, here's the Count.

ADRIEN

Well, since he's seen you together, begin to play your role of a fool. Turn your back on Nanette like an oaf. You, Nanette, modestly lower your eyes—and go away by that side.

(Exit Nanette. Enter the Count.)

COUNT

What's the intrigue going on here?

ADRIEN (laughing)

Ha, ha, ha, sir. It's the funniest thing in the world. You see this moron who's gaping idly? He's the most pleasant (changing to a serious tone) original. First of all, I must tell you he's my relative. The young farmer I proposed to you the other day.

COUNT

Fine, but what's he doing with Nanette?

ADRIEN (laughing)

Ha, ha, ha. That's what's so funny. (seriously) I'm going to tell you. I am going to tell you he'll take your farm without bargaining—and Nanette without money for (laughing) the honor of your protection. But, what's so funny is that I wanted to allure him with Nanette's charms. Not at all. He's not interested in beauty, he says—all faces are the same to him.

COUNT

That's funny enough. But, what do you prove by that?

ADRIEN

I prove that here's a husband like we need for Nanette—without love, without jealousy—who won't even care that his wife was with the Great Lord.

COUNT

Indeed, he seems to me to be a big baby.

ADRIEN

Right! An idiot, in fact. He will be docile, humble, respectful of your rank, and he will have a blind and affectionate confidence in you and his wife.

COUNT

I don't intend to abuse it. I love Nanette only for her wit—for her conversation.

ADRIEN

I know that perfectly, sir, but you won't allow yourself to be angry when a jealous husband comes to interrupt you while you were by way of saying pretty things.

COUNT

It's not a question of that, but let's see if this boy here will accommodate me anyway for my farm.

ADRIEN

Approach, Cousin Bertram, approach.

DORANTE (in a naïve tone)

What do you want, cousin?

ADRIEN

Greet the count. Go on, greet him.

COUNT

Hello, my boy, hello. Your cousin says you want to be my farmer.

DORANTE

If it's your pleasure, milord. I ask your pardon for that.

COUNT (to Adrien)

He's really stupid.

ADRIEN

I've told my cousin the price of your farm. He agrees to everything and will give more than twenty gold crowns worth of wine.

COUNT

On your account, Adrien, I am listening to his proposals, but someone has to reply to me.

DORANTE

I have a good answer then.

COUNT

Hey, who is it?

DORANTE

Oh, damn, I'm going to reach you my answer.

COUNT (laughing)

Reach me his answer. What an imbecile.

DORANTE

Hey, yeah. For my answer is in my pocket. He's a better answerer than money, for when he answers, he pays, he pays.

COUNT

He has some wit, this guy here.

DORANTE

Here already, the wine to drink, milord. For you to drink, and then here's a hoard of money that I made in my last farm, and this will serve to pay you in advance—in advance—it's a trick I have for being sooner quits.

COUNT

The manners of this man agree with me well enough. I hope he'll agree with Nanette.

DORANTE

Who's this Nanette? Is it that little slip of a girl I saw there?

COUNT

Yes. Don't you find her pretty?

DORANTE

Yes, she's what you call pretty right enough, but as for me, I don't aspire to the attractive girls, for what I need is no trouble. You see, all my pleasure is in making a farm really pay.

COUNT

Won't you consent to take her for your wife?

DORANTE

Hey, if it's your pleasure that I take her, I'll take her alright.

COUNT

His willingness delights me.

DORANTE

But, at least on the condition she doesn't get too passionately fond around me, for I don't care to be interrupted when I work. I will do my little thing on the one side, she on the other. That's freedom which makes for peace in a good household.

COUNT

He's right.

DORANTE

By the way, milord, I was forgetting to tell you of a thing—it's that I have to take little trips to my province from time to time.

COUNT

Oh, I intend you to be sedentary.

DORANTE

Oh, I cannot. But I will leave my wife in my place to make sure you are satisfied.

COUNT

In that case, I prefer to suffer with it a bit.

ADRIEN

The Count is such a good master.

COUNT

Still, Adrien, to be able to have the marriage in peace, we have to make the Countess believe that this man will take Nanette far away. (to Dorante) That's because my wife doesn't like to see her.

ADRIEN

Let me inform the Countess. I take it on myself to obtain her consent.

COUNT

Here she is. I am going to pay her a compliment with this news.

(Enter Countess.)

COUNTESS (in a fury)

Lucas has just told me that he never will marry Nanette and as for me, I tell you plainly that I am going to shut her in a—

COUNT

Easy, easy. Let's forget the little altercation we had. My action is going to stop your mouth and dissipate your fears. It's not enough to be faithful, one must even exhaust one's imagination to eliminate the least suspicions of jealousy. So, as to satisfy you, I am giving Nanette to this young lover who will take her away tomorrow, and I will give my farm to Lucas on the condition that he remain a bachelor.

COUNTESS

If there's no trickery in what you tell me—how sweet.

COUNT

You like the proposal? Are you satisfied?

COUNTESS

God is not pleased for me to contradict you in any way. I will do what you wish as soon as you perform what you have promised me.

COUNT

We'll settle the other business tomorrow. Today we'll think only of the marriage.

COUNTESS

Let's first assure ourselves that the farm goes to Lucas.

COUNT

I beg you—begin by signing the contract.

COUNTESS

I beg you—begin with the lease.

COUNT

Is it that you don't trust me?

COUNTESS

Would you deceive me?

COUNT

No, but I insist on a blind trust.

COUNTESS

And, as for me, I insist on seeing clearly. You intend for Nanette to remain here.

COUNT

Oh! She will stay here, if it pleases me. Do you dare to contradict me?

COUNTESS

Do you dare to offend me so?

COUNT

Don't push me past the limit.

COUNTESS

Don't burn my ears.

COUNT

By God!

COUNTESS

Death of my life.

COUNT

I don't know what prevents me—

ADRIEN (low)

Hey, sir, go away. Leave it to me to make her see reason.

COUNT

I am going to get the Notary to come. And if you don't sign—I will separate from you—from bed and board, from bed and board.

ADRIEN (signaling the Countess not to reply)

I will easily prevent this divorce.

(Exit the Count.)

ADRIEN

Hey, Madame—just now I signaled you to consent to everything.

COUNTESS

Me—consent!

ADRIEN

In your interest, I've dreamed up a stratagem to deceive the Count. I was going to tell you.

COUNTESS

Yeah. What were you going to tell me?

ADRIEN

That this man is not a farmer. That he's a rich gentleman in love with Nanette—who has disguised himself to take her away—with your consent.

COUNTESS

Are you telling me the truth?

ADRIEN

I am going to make you see he has only the outer shell of a peasant. Here, Madame.

(Adrien opens Dorante's overcoat to reveal a magnificent vest.)

DORANTE

You can make my happiness, madame, and yours, also, by giving me Nanette.

COUNTESS

But, you are not deceiving me? For one can still borrow a vest.

DORANTE

Here's a watch worth sixty crowns that I beg you to accept as a proof of my good faith.

COUNTESS (taking the watch and softening up)

One can also borrow a watch, but one cannot borrow the air of nobility and gallantry with which you do things. I swear to you, sir, that if I accept your watch, it's to persuade you, I believe you are a great lord.

DORANTE

Very happy you have such confidence in me.

ADRIEN

Here's the Count coming back. Pretend nothing has happened.

(Enter the Count with Nanette.)

COUNT

The Notary is on my heels, Madame, and we are going to see if I am the master. Come, Nanette, I order you to love this man here.

NANETTE

You are the master, sir, and I will obey you.

COUNT

Yes, wife, I am the master and I know how to make you see reason.

COUNTESS

Alas! That is not reason—it's love which conquers me. You threatened me with divorce—to separate from you, my dear husband! Oh, rather death.

COUNT

You make me feel tender when you no longer contradict me.

COUNTESS

I ask your pardon for my bluntness.

COUNTESS

I was the one who got a bit carried away.

COUNTESS

People accuse women of beginning these quarrels. But they are also the first to stop. I've always had a special tenderness for you.

COUNT

I will inform you in the future—but I beg you.

COUNTESS

Ah, don't finish. My compliance would be imperfect, if you had only the trouble of repeating your intentions to me. You wish this boy to marry Nanette, that he be your farmer, that she be your concierge. I consent to it willingly.

COUNT

What goodness, what wifely goodness! Go, I will repay you for it. You understand, Bertram, the Countess gives you Nanette in marriage. May you cherish each other as tenderly as we cherish each other, my wife and I.

ADRIEN

You have before your eyes a beautiful example of unity.

(Enter Lucas and his Mother.)

LUCAS

Count, here's the wedding I bring you, as you've ordered me. My Mother told me to put love in a jug. That's the long and short of it.

MOTHER

Ha, ha, is this the new fiancée? He's got a smoother face than my son. Nanette will like him better.

COUNT

Let's go in to sign the contract and we will return after we celebrate. Let's begin soon.

(Exit all but Lucas, his Mother, and Adrien.)

ADRIEN

You are, indeed, lucky, Mr. Lucas, for having avoided the inconveniences of marrying—for they had already put you in the village Vaudeville where they sing about all the new marriages. Wait, wait—do you hear them?

(The Wedding Guests enter and the violins lay the Vaudeville as Adrien sings the words.)

ADRIEN (singing)

Pal Gervais

Got nothing

From the Lord of the Manor.

Neither wife, nor farm

Nor money.

He took from your household

Ruin in a rage

And took at your expense

On your wife and heirs

Engrafted large interests.

Drunken throngs

Don't go looking

Where your wife is going

Dining with a young neighbor.

Don't ask if you drink the

Wine he gives you.

Just have a junket,

Carouse around.

Soon, as you entrap

His bond of wine

You'll find your honor with

The lees.

(to an old man)

Old Papa Lucas,

You tell me confidentially,

You're growing younger.

With a young serving girl,

You want to keep her

Jumping, fiery, prancing.

You don't understand her.

The more your

Wife is frolicsome,

The less you are likely to live.

Don't kid yourself

That with flattery

You'll make yourself

Young again.

For, with you grumbling disposition,

Grunting and sneaking,

Be sure that

The younger your wife is,

The shorter you'll live.

(The Count returns with the Countess and the others.)

COUNT

Well, gang, the wedding is not going to be broken off. The contract is signed and we will think only of celebrating.

(They sing)

Honor and homage

Are due the Lord of the Manor.

But by mischance

He often demands

From the wisest tenant

Honor and the first right.

(They dance)

As for me,

I don't want

My wife to advance

Too near the lords

Who make advances.

That's troublesome at night,

For in making her curtsy,

She might make a faux pas.

(Dorante enters, dressed decently, and Adrien follows in Dorante's livery.)

DORANTE

Sir, I acted the peasant to obtain Nanette, I return as a gentleman to thank you.

COUNT

I am deceived! Vassals, servants—help me!

ADRIEN

You have no other vassal than me, and I am now this gentleman's vassal.

COUNTESS

We've been duped, my lamb, but console yourself. If they've run off with Nanette, you'll find in me a legitimate consolation.

(They dance.)

ADRIEN (singing)

The road is open

For those lucky lackeys

Who wait on gentlemen.

But to complete their career

I don't see what step

Is to be taken.

For an innocent shepherdess

The voyage is great

From village to palace,

From the palace

To the isle of Venus.

I don't see what step

Is to be taken.

From the spirit

Simple and democratic,

To the spirit

Sublime and knowledgeable,

The voyage is long

From wit to fancy.

I don't see what step

Is to be taken.

In the ardent desire

To satisfy you

The way is more difficult.

It seems easy to us,

But to know how to please

I don't know what step

Is to be taken.

CURTAIN

ABOUT THE TRANSLATOR

Frank J. Morlock has written and translated many plays since retiring from the legal profession in 1992. His translations have also appeared on Project Gutenberg, the Alexandre Dumas Père web page, Literature in the Age of Napoléon, Infinite Artistries. com, and Munsey's (formerly Blackmask). In 2006 he received an award from the North American Jules Verne Society for his translations of Verne's plays. He lives and works in México.

www.ingramcontent.com/pod-product-compliance
Lightning Source LLC
LaVergne TN
LVHW041627070426
835507LV00008B/497